Mill Spit

poems by

Alexandra Kemrer

Finishing Line Press
Georgetown, Kentucky

Mill Spit

All that is gold does not glitter; not all those who wander are lost;
the old that is strong does not wither;
deep roots are not reached by the frost.

—J.R.R. Tolkien

ACKNOWLEDGMENTS

Rune Literary Journal 2018: "Shift Change" and "Mill Kids"
Voices from the Attic, Vol. XXIV: "A Girl Ago" and "He Grew up Fatherless"

This collection of poems would not have been written without the Madwomen
writing program at Carlow University under the direction of the renowned
poet, Jan Beatty. As a result of her vision and constant dedication, accomplished
poets helped me find the courage and develop the skills I needed to write.

I thank Nancy Kygrowski who opened my heart and mind that had been
waiting for years to write poetry. I thank my mentors who kept me writing
and revising, Kayla Sargeson, Liane Norman, Diane Kerr, and Emily Mohn-
Slate. I want to especially thank my most recent mentors, Diane and Emily,
who pushed me to complete this collection of poems and to submit them for
publication.

Thank you to Katie Henry who provided valuable feedback and support
whenever I asked, and a very special thank you to my dear friend and "sister,"
Julie Cecchini, who persuaded me to take my first writing class at Carlow.

Finally, I must acknowledge my precious grandchildren, Elise, Katherine,
Quinn, Grant, and Claire; they are members of the world's family of children
who deserve our very best efforts to ensure the air they breathe is clean.

Publisher: Leah Maines
Editor: Christen Kincaid
Cover Art: Alexandra Kemrer
Author Photo: Alexandra Kemrer
Cover Design: Leah Huete

Printed in the USA on acid-free paper.
Order online: www.finishinglinepress.com
also available on amazon.com

Author inquiries and mail orders:
Finishing Line Press
P. O. Box 1626
Georgetown, Kentucky 40324
U. S. A.

Table of Contents

Shift Change

men pour out of the mill gates at the end of each shift
seven in the morning   eleven at night

a mumbling bass sound proclaims their coming
tidal wave of men
         raccoon eyes
            hunched backs
               slumped shoulders
bruised lunch pails

men slowly disappear into worn buildings that wait
stoically opposite the iron mill gate

Sons of Italy
Polish Falcons
Russian Pol. & Ben. Club

sooted black outside
flashing neon inside

shove up to the bar
rail of communion

        Gimme a shot 'na beer!!

steel grit   pig iron chalk coal dust
stuck on skin inside
jaws down
throats around

   teeth
     & tongues

sharp whisky dislodges mill leftovers
Iron City follows fast gathering up everything in its path

How's your ol' lady?
Same.
How's yours?
Same.

Mill Spit

is in the air
sticking to window sills
lying on clothes lines
clinging to work shirts
graying street lamps

i play in a vacant lot
a street up from the mill
humming   skipping
waving my bent spoon
ready for digging

i force my spoon
into the ground
scoop up a clump
of bright yellow dirt

stings my tongue
bitterbitterbitter
icky   greasy
prickly going down

a shiny black ribbon
curls through the yellow
i save a spoonful
carry it home to mom

fancy butter   i call it
mom calls it   *mill spit*
she can't explain the yellow

Yellow, Not Inglorious

Yellowjacket or *meat bee*
genus: mystery

flight patterns undrawn
              ground crews unseen

buzzing   tsimmering

stringy forearms curl
              in nested moldy leaves

black and butter ally   day's firefly
              clips thistle tips   till summer wanes

where do they go?

daisy chain of fathers' hands
              calloused pads grasp hot steel

shredded   leathery singed

at night cracked yellow palms   press
              together to pray   seared fingers quake

When Soot Owns the Air

When soot owns the air, you rely on
the memory of steps, how many it
takes to walk from your door to the
curb, then across the street, the
number of steps in the next block,
then across the next street. When
soot covers you and surrounds you,
looking down at your feet is the
safest way to walk.

Staircase to School

one step
two steps
crumbling edges
four
count the steps
up the hill
hill too steep for cars

short step
high step
slanted step
missing step
count the steps
down the hill
hill too steep for cars

wet step
icy step
snowy step
slushy step
crunchy step
up the hill
hill too steep for cars

wobbly step
tip gone step
watch them steps
one hundred
thirty-two steps
down the hill
hill too steep for cars

drumming steps
dumbing steps
concreak steps
cracked block steps
thicker wicked steps
slam & damn the steps
hill too steep for cars

If

eye level to my bedroom
a practice room across the street
two brick apartment buildings'
windows open to each other

little girls   my size
tutued   pink shoed
pony tails flipping
(I have one too)

satin toes pad-padding
across a wooden floor
the clink-edged tune
from an old upright piano

I close my window.

If I catch you dancing
I'll break your legs;
you're a mill kid,
my father said.

Sunday at St. John's Episcopal

The Baptist blesses us
from a stain glass window
edged with purple
vines bursting grapes.

On either side, half-open
flowered windows
invite smoggy summer
air into the choir stall.

I am singing in the pew,
dressed in my handsewn
black muslin robe
so long it rests on my feet.

I faint from the stifling heat
filling the space between
the heavy robe
and my little body.

Grown-up communicants
in fine hats and ties
wait for me to rise again,
to kneel, to stand,

to sing my favorite
children's hymn:

I sing a song
of the saints of God,
For the saints of God
are just folk like me,
and I mean to be one too.

A Porch

juts out
above
a broken

concrete
path
leading

to an
abandoned
mill

beside
a black
river

wood
almost
square

small
grayed
bare

peppery
brick
wall

hardly
visible
door

wilted
brown
frame

paint
crackled
shedding

faded
American
flag

stuck
behind
rusted light

The Stick

I feel the stick in my pocket, silky
from petting. I stroke it as I search
concrete curbs for the best spot.

I bend over each section that looks
promising. It has to be just the right
height and solid.

The curb I used last week won't work.
Pebbly bits tumbled onto the street.
Too much soot.

I keep looking, examining edges,
the stick in my pocket getting smoother.
I feel it.

Suddenly, I see the best spot.
I take my stick, set it down carefully
between the curb and the street.

Stiff backed, the stick's head lays
on the sidewalk edge, its feet
firmly planted on the street.

I'm an animal eyeing my target.
The drum roll begins,
fills my mind, vibrates my body.

I pull my right leg back, bend
my waist forward, curve my neck.
I explode!

Like a dream ballerina, my bare thigh
rises high, higher, my toe's tip
kicks the stick with perfect power!

My stick soars!
Squinty eyed, I follow the arc
of my stick flying though the smog.

It falls, lands   unbroken
waits for me on the blackened street.

Donora, Pennsylvania, 1948

hopscotch   white chalk
black sooted   side walk

all around the mulberry bush
the monkey chased the weasel

U.S. Steel
American Steel and Wire Plant
Zinc Plant

the monkey thought 'twas all in fun

I lean out my bedroom window
strain to see the street below.

Doc Brown bends over a man
lying down, back on the sidewalk.

I've no time to laugh or cry

He places his hand above
the man's open mouth, then

slowly, gently, pulls wrinkled
eye lids over water filled eyes.

A Girl Ago
—after Lucie Brock-Broido

a stuffed kitten sleeps on my pillow
muffed paws curled under her belly

her plump and chubby cheeks
smooshed against mine

paper dolls crisp and muted
flown all the way from Europe

to "the little girl with skinned
knees who loves butter"

sent by a soldier the uncle
I would never see

Lisa's long black hair sweeps
the dirt off jagged cement

our upside down inside knees
curl around scratchy metal bars

we don't talk about her dad
the mill tragedy

alone
in the apartment
by the mill

where war needy steel
rolls out metal sheets

I hide pennies
hide them
                                        where
no one can see

                    behind pictures   on door frames

pretend they are gone

                                          then find them
                                                hide them

        find them again

He Grew Up Fatherless

My father always promised me that we would live in France.
We'd go boating on the Seine, and I would learn to dance.
                    —Judy Collins

too soon widowed mom
six children
single room

not a speck of dirt
raised skinny chickens
picked stunted fruit

sliced narrow noodle strips
kneaded daily bread
warm bowlfuls of soup

after thanks were fed
boys worked odd jobs
instead of kid's play

Grandma said
'member boys
no doc   no pay

plain dishes done
cupboarded away
all knelt
by handmade beds
whispered
Lord's Prayer

as one
in their native
Slavonic tongue

17

No Slide Rules Need Apply

Starky said he heard Mr. Hoosac talking
about something called a slide rule.

It looked like a ruler but was a lot fancier
and could figure out math problems really fast.

So, we talked to Mr. Hoosac who agreed to teach
us after school if the principal said it was ok.

We made an appointment with Mr. Joyba,
enthusiastically presented our case,
talking over each other.

It seemed ages before Mr. Hoosac
finally called us into his classroom.
He wouldn't meet our eyes.

My stomach turned queasy.
Mr. Hoosac said, *I'm sorry, kids.*
Mr. Joyba felt it was too dangerous.

My Piano Closet

A Symphony in Five Movements

I

Two burly men carry the piano
up creaking apartment steps,
down the narrow hall.

The black upright squeals
as they push it across
the bare floor into the closet.

No longer hidden
by over-stuffed boxes,
a small window lets light in.

Just 25.00, church organist
smiles. Dad's lips turn down.
I don't know who paid.

II

88 tulips planted in a box
white tulips with tips pale yellow

like fingers that held
too many Pall Malls

among the white tulips
tipped with pale yellow

are black slivered planks
with edges worn gray

like palms that have gripped
too many steel pails

sweaty fingers in summer
cover white tulips with dew

chilly fingers in winter warm
when they slide & staccato

Interlude

Can you enclose wilderness in a raised boxed bed?

III

sonatinas and arpeggios
small fingers stroke keys
scherzo andante

allegro with feeling
hammer down
then ease

fall leaves tinkling
holiday tunes
spring recital in bloom

Schumann's
Kinderszenen
childhood scenes

IV

smoggy light filters in
plunky sounds slip out
swing your partner
'round about

under my window
on the street outside
brown shirted men women
in doily collared frocks pass by

they smile and sway
to concerts performed
by the magnificent
black box and I

V

I wasn't supposed to like music
but I did.
I wasn't supposed to hear music
but I did
I wasn't supposed to play music
but I did.

My Saints are Broken

would you take

an English sparrow

clasp her tightly

in your left hand

beak open

squeaking

grip the scissors

in your right hand

approach her body

and deliberately

slowly

clip

each soft

feathered

wing

one by one

would you

Lush Life

Take it.
Please.
Take it.

Plump raspberries
        wait for picking.

Place them in your mouth,
all of them.
Slide them along the slick skin
        of your inside cheek.
Smoosh them against your milk teeth,
succulent   red.
                What is the color of red?

132 Stone Steps to School

I walk you
all of you
4 times a day
5 days a week

up to school
in the morning
back home
in the afternoon

up to school
after lunch
home when
school is done

this last walk
is the best
it's up to me now
I take my time

I sit on a step
look down below
at the bottom
the beginning

rows of black
buildings line
either side
of the street

homey rooms
sweet smells
dinner cooking
aproned wives

mill workers
waking up
getting ready
for their shifts

short walk to gate
from these apartments
that lean forward
slant towards

the plants   spitting up
smoke & red flames
stretched out along
the Monongahela

even from way up here
I still can't see the river

The Mill

you were hard
hot
dangerous
you took men
made steel
you didn't know
children
mothers
you didn't care
that you didn't know
you took fathers
husbands
sons
you made steel

What Becomes

White shirt sleeves rolled to her elbows
each school day she entered our room
prepared to teach us mill kids Latin.

We thought she was very odd.
If Ichabod Crane had a sister,
that would be Miss Ewing:
short cropped hair,
straight black skirt,
tall rigid body.

She paced back and forth
across the front of the classroom,
bending slightly forward from the waist,
mumbling an internal dialogue,
frowning and shaking her head:

What will become of them?
So much ignorance.

After school, I knocked on her door.

What seems to be the problem? she said.

I heard what you said in class and I don't want to be ignorant.
Can you help me? I said.

Oh my...wait a minute.

She took a piece of paper from her desk and began writing,

A list of books.
She told me to get one from our town library,
then come back to see her.

Crime and Punishment sounded exciting.
I walked to the library.
The librarian said, *there is no such book,*
and gave me another one she thought
my teacher meant instead, which I read.

I returned to Miss Ewing's classroom.

*Why on earth did you read that book
and not one on the list I gave you?*

Filled with shame,
I whispered, *I wanted to read Crime and Punishment
but the librarian said there was no such book.*

Miss Ewing softened, said she would bring me the books.

They Say

They say you can be anything you want to be.

They say always listen to your elders.

They say youth is wasted on the young.

They say keep your powder dry.

They say trauma to a child continues into adulthood.

They say you can't go home again.

They say the apple never falls far from the tree.

They say children should be seen and not heard.

They say you never know until you try.

They say shit happens and then you die.

They say for every pot there's a lid.

They say wisdom is female. He disagrees.

They say bad luck comes in threes.

They say the world's your oyster.

What's an oyster? asks the mill kid.

Mill Kids

Sonya's last name is Garcia
but we pronounce it "Garsha"
I don't know why

Sonya attempted suicide
they said it was pills
I don't know why

we're classmates 12 yrs old
we live in apartments
near the Mon river above the mills

we live at opposite ends
of the mile long charcoal stick
my family by the open hearth
Sonya's family by the zinc

puffs of mill smoke surround us
we smell sulfur   breathe smog
I don't know why

her hospital room is dim
window curtains drawn
a single high bed
wooden night stand
no chairs

I stand at the foot of her bed
and in my small voice say
Hello Sonya
are you ok

she pulls the white sheet
up just over her chin
then turns her head
to one side   away

her silence owns the room

I'm sorry I say
I hope you get ok

I Am a Girl Folded

in half, backwards, my under-knees rough as rusty bars.
My lioness' mane scratches concrete as I swing like a simian
over worn out steps edging towards the basement door,
the basement door that hides our coal-fired hearth, controlled
violence, like the steel mill's insides down by the river.

Broken legs don't dance. Sea legs do.
I am sea life, waving and curling.
I hide pennies and find them and hide them again.
I always look down when walking. I might find an empty
Lucky Strike pack on the sidewalk and stomp on it for good luck.
And I count the steps to school, hoping the number will change.

Notes

"Donora, Pennsylvania, 1948" is based on an historical event. For 5 days (Oct. 27-31), the mill town suffered deadly air pollution. The everyday polluted air, a mixture of hydrogen fluoride and sulfur dioxide emissions from U.S. Steel's plants, was trapped over the town by a temperature inversion. Twenty people died suddenly and at least 50 more residents died from respiratory distress within the next month. *The New York Times* described it as "one of the worst air pollution disasters in the nation's history" (Nov. 1, 2008).

Alexandra Kemrer first began writing poetry in the Madwomen's writing program at Carlow University after pursuing careers in French language and literature, archaeology and law. Her hometown of Donora, Pennsylvania, and the people who lived in the smoggy mill town, kept appearing in her writing so she decided to try capturing that period in a collection of poems. Her debut chapbook, *Mill Spit*, is a testament to the hardships and character of the immigrant families who lived in mill towns during the early years of the industrial revolution in Southwestern Pennsylvania. It is her hope that these poems will contribute to a more personal understanding of the effect unchecked pollution has on children's and adults' lives. "We must do better for the coming generations," she warns.

Kemrer's poems have appeared in *Voices from the Attic, Rune,* and Pittsburgh City Paper's *Chapter and Verse*. She lives and writes in Pittsburgh, PA and is currently working on a full length book of poems.

www.ingramcontent.com/pod-product-compliance
Lightning Source LLC
LaVergne TN
LVHW051611080426
835510LV00020B/3233